CHI

LIBRARY Hounslow C

FOCUS ON

TREES

Anita Ganeri

D0509996

This edition published 2003
© Aladdin Books Ltd 2003

All rights reserved

Designed and produced by
Aladdin Books Ltd
28 Percy Street
London W1T 2BZ

First published in
Great Britain in 1993 by
Watts Books
96 Leonard Street
London EC2A 4XD

ISBN 0 7496 5378 7

A catalogue record for this book is
available from the British Library.

Printed in UAE

Design	David West Children's Book Design
Designer	Flick Killerby
Series director	Bibby Whittaker
Editor	Elise Bradbury
Picture research	Emma Krikler
Illustrators	Rob Shone Adrian Lascom, Garden Studios

The author, Anita Ganeri, has written
many books for children on natural history
and other topics.

The educational consultant, Fiona Christie,
has been a primary school teacher for
several years in New Zealand and Britain.

The consultant, Steve Parker, has a first
class honours degree in science. He is an
experienced author, editor and consultant
on science and nature books.

INTRODUCTION

Trees are one of the Earth's greatest natural resources. For thousands of years people have relied on them for food, wood and shelter. Ancient Scandinavian peoples even believed that their gods created the first human beings from trees. This book provides the science to understand trees, and also links them with information about history and literature, maths projects, geographical facts and arts activities. The key below shows how the subjects are divided up. We hope that the following projects help you to develop your own ways of discovering trees.

Geography

The symbol of the planet Earth shows where geographical facts and activities, like map making, are included. Because there is growing concern about the state of the environment, facts on green issues are highlighted with a green symbol.

Language and literature

An open book is the sign for activities which involve language. These will explore how words are derived from the world around us. Activities also include examining how trees and forests are portrayed in films and literature.

Science
The microscope symbol indicates a science project or experiment, or where scientific information is given. If the symbol is tinted green it signals an environmental issue.

History
The sign of the scroll and hourglass shows where historical information is given. These sections explore how people have used trees and wood through the ages, and encourage questioning about the past.

Maths
Maths projects are indicated by the symbol of a ruler and compass. Activities involve measuring, estimating, and comparing sizes. These projects will use maths to increase knowledge about trees.

Arts, crafts and music
The symbol showing a sheet of music and art tools signals arts, crafts or musical activities. Many imaginative things can be done with leaves, nuts and other products from trees. Projects include practical crafts, like making paper, and also more artistic creations.

CONTENTS

2/04
CHISWICK LIBRARY
C 2124166

WHAT ARE TREES?

A tree is a type of plant, but with a difference. Unlike other plants, trees have tall, strong trunks made of wood. Most trees grow over six metres tall. They are divided into three main groups – conifers, broadleaves and palms. The first trees grew on Earth about 300 million years ago. From fossil evidence, they seem to have been types of conifers, similar to spruces and pines.

Douglas fir cone and branch

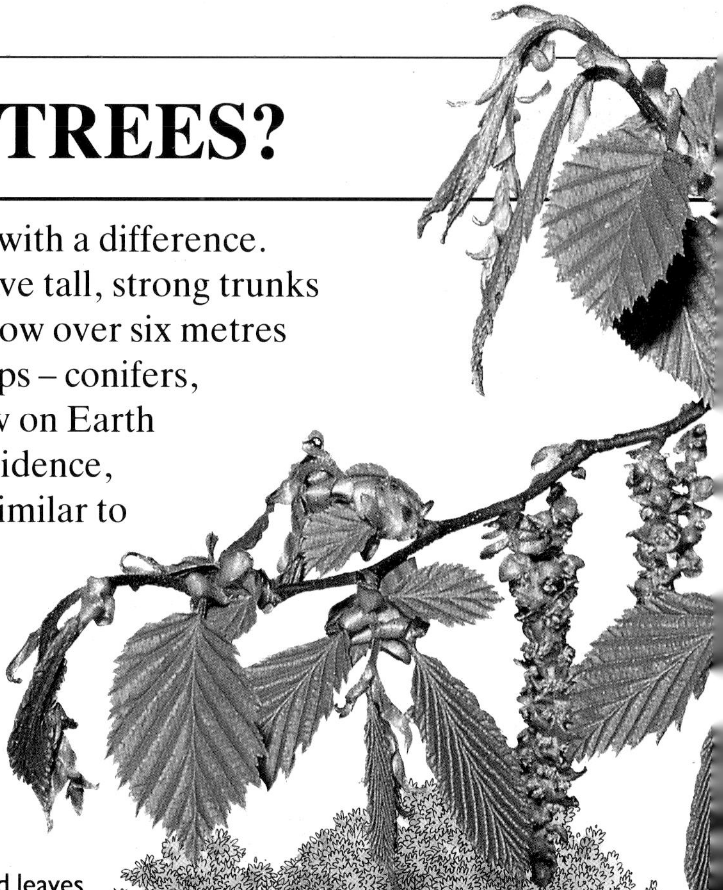

Hornbeam blossoms and leaves

Conifer: Douglas fir

Broadleaf: Hornbeam

Conifers

Most conifers have needle-like or scaly leaves and produce woody cones instead of fruit. Many have a pyramid shape, and almost all are evergreens – they keep their leaves all year round.

Broadleaves

Most broadleaved trees have flat, wide leaves. Many are deciduous, which means they shed their leaves in winter. All broadleaf trees produce flowers, and fruits containing seeds.

Tree symbols

Nations adopt designs for their flags which symbolise an important aspect of the country. Some nations which have chosen trees or leaves to represent them are shown here. How else are trees used as symbols?

Lebanon
The cedar of Lebanon has been a symbol of the region since Biblical times.

Haiti
The flag of Haiti has a palm tree at its centre because many palms grow there.

Canada
The maple leaf which adorns Canada's flag was adopted because sugar maples are common in the east of the country.

Cyprus
The olive branches on Cyprus's flag symbolise peace. Olive trees grow in many Mediterranean lands.

Equatorial Guinea
This small country on the west coast of Africa displays its native silk cotton tree on the national flag.

Chusan palm fronds

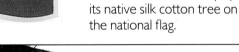

Identifying types

Each species of tree has a particular silhouette. To identify a tree, draw its shape in a notebook. Write down any other details, like the shape and colour of its leaves, the environment it grows in, and describe its flowers, fruit and bark. Then compare your notes with a tree identification book to find out what kind of tree it is.

Maple

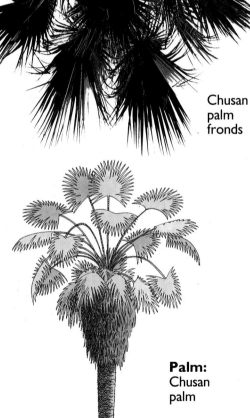

Palm: Chusan palm

Palms

Unlike other trees, palms only grow upwards, not outwards. This is because they do not make proper wood to widen their trunks (see page 21). Instead of bark, tough fibres protect their stalk-like trunks.

LEAVES

The number of leaves a tree has varies from species to species and from season to season. Pine trees may have millions of needles. A large oak tree may have about 250,000 leaves. But all leaves do the same jobs. They make food for the tree by photosynthesis. They also have tiny holes found mainly on their undersides, called stomata. Trees breathe through these holes and also lose water through them, in a process called transpiration.

Leaves come in a huge range of shapes and sizes. The needles or scaly leaves of most conifers are easy to recognise. The leaves of broadleaved trees are divided into two main types. Simple leaves have a single leaf blade attached to the leaf stalk. Compound leaves are made up of several small leaflets. The leaf edge, or margin, may be smooth, lobed or jagged.

Leaf stalk (petiole)

Veins carry food and water around the leaf and strengthen it, like a skeleton.

Leaf point (apex)

Main leaf vein (midrib)

Leaf edge (margin)

BIG TOOTH ASPEN LEAF

Measuring area
If two shapes are different it can be difficult to tell which has a larger surface area. To compare the sizes of two leaves, use a piece of graph paper and trace around each leaf. Count the number of squares inside the outlines. Then measure one square and multiply the number of squares inside each shape by this measurement. Will leaves from the same tree have the same area?

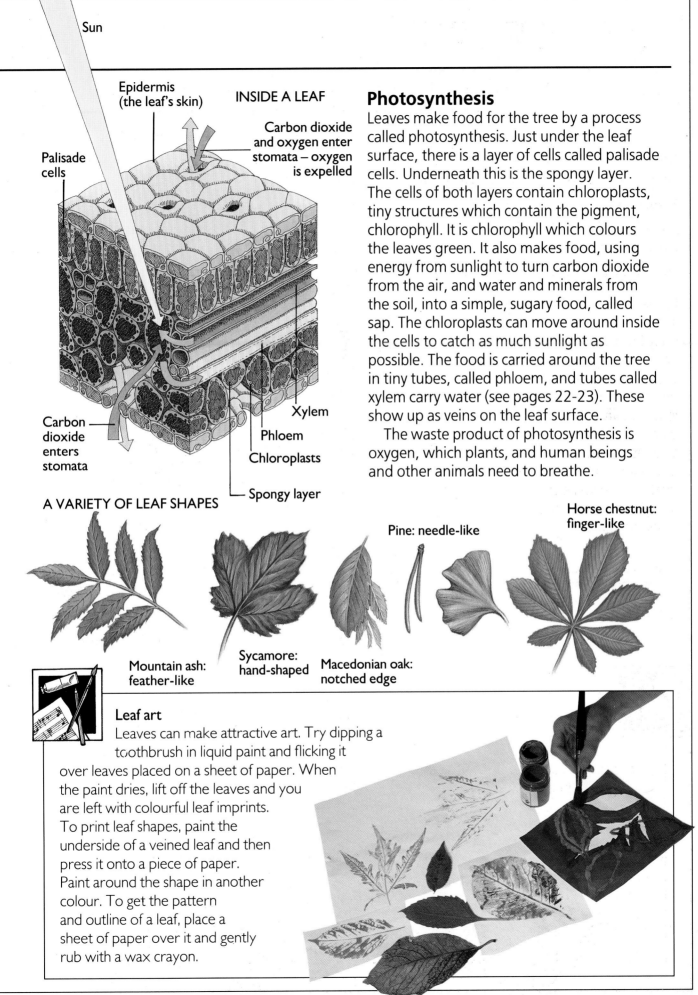

Sun

Epidermis
(the leaf's skin)

INSIDE A LEAF

Palisade
cells

Carbon dioxide
and oxygen enter
stomata – oxygen
is expelled

Carbon
dioxide
enters
stomata

Xylem

Phloem

Chloroplasts

Spongy layer

A VARIETY OF LEAF SHAPES

Mountain ash:
feather-like

Sycamore:
hand-shaped

Macedonian oak:
notched edge

Pine: needle-like

Horse chestnut:
finger-like

Photosynthesis

Leaves make food for the tree by a process called photosynthesis. Just under the leaf surface, there is a layer of cells called palisade cells. Underneath this is the spongy layer. The cells of both layers contain chloroplasts, tiny structures which contain the pigment, chlorophyll. It is chlorophyll which colours the leaves green. It also makes food, using energy from sunlight to turn carbon dioxide from the air, and water and minerals from the soil, into a simple, sugary food, called sap. The chloroplasts can move around inside the cells to catch as much sunlight as possible. The food is carried around the tree in tiny tubes, called phloem, and tubes called xylem carry water (see pages 22-23). These show up as veins on the leaf surface.

The waste product of photosynthesis is oxygen, which plants, and human beings and other animals need to breathe.

Leaf art

Leaves can make attractive art. Try dipping a toothbrush in liquid paint and flicking it over leaves placed on a sheet of paper. When the paint dries, lift off the leaves and you are left with colourful leaf imprints. To print leaf shapes, paint the underside of a veined leaf and then press it onto a piece of paper. Paint around the shape in another colour. To get the pattern and outline of a leaf, place a sheet of paper over it and gently rub with a wax crayon.

DECIDUOUS & EVERGREEN

Deciduous trees lose their leaves in winter for the same reason that animals hibernate – to save energy and survive the cold. When the temperature falls, roots of deciduous trees cannot draw in much water from the cold soil. If the leaves stayed on the tree, they would lose water through transpiration which would not be replenished. This would kill the tree. Evergreen trees keep their leaves all year round. A tough, waxy covering limits water loss and protects leaves from the drying effects of the wind.

An evergreen holly leaf in winter

A deciduous hawthorn leaf in autumn

In autumn, many deciduous trees become a blaze of colour – russet, red, yellow and maroon. This is because the balance of pigments (colourings) inside each leaf changes. As the leaves die, the green pigment, chlorophyll, breaks down. Other pigments, which are usually hidden by the chlorophyll, now show through.

Seasonal changes

One way to tell if a tree is deciduous is to observe it through the changing seasons. Most conifers are evergreens, but the larch is an exception. When the weather turns cold, its needles die and fall off. Keep a record of how and when deciduous trees change throughout the year.

Spring   Summer   Autumn   Winter

Tree survey

Making a map is one way you can record the kinds of trees growing in an area. Using a piece of plain or graph paper, draw in landmarks like streets or buildings. Try to keep to scale, and locate on your map all the deciduous and evergreen trees you see.

Make up other symbols for anything else you want to put on your map. Create a key to show what the symbols stand for. If you want to make a more detailed map showing species of trees, use a tree identification book and make different symbols for each kind of tree you observe. What are the most common trees in your area?

KEY

■ DECIDUOUS

■ EVERGREEN

■ BUILDING

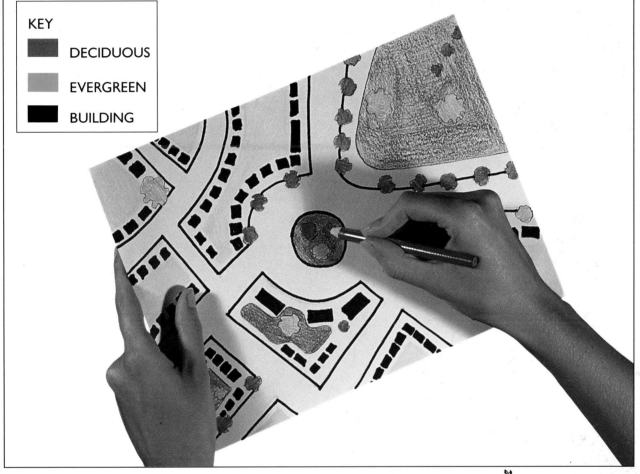

Deep in the forest...

Many stories portray forests as frightening places, or places where magical things happen. In **The Wizard of Oz** the trees in the wood come alive – with evil intentions towards Dorothy and her friends. **The Hobbit** travels through a dangerous forest, but is saved by the Ents – tree people with magical qualities. Shakespeare's **A Midsummer Night's Dream** is set in a forest with a fairy queen who turns the head of a weaver named Bottom into a donkey's head. How are woods and trees written about in books you have read?

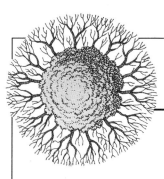

ROOTS

Tree roots do two main jobs. They anchor the tree firmly in the ground, so that it is not easily blown over by the wind. They also draw up water and minerals from the soil, which the leaves need to make food. Some roots grow very deep into the ground. Most, however, branch and spread outwards to anchor the tree more securely. This also means that the roots can collect water and minerals from a wide area.

ROOT SYSTEM OF A TREE

Root tip

CROSS-SECTION
OF A ROOT TIP

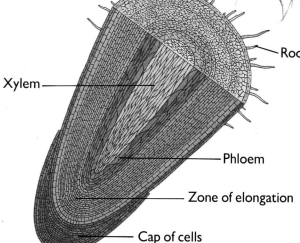

Root hair

Xylem

Phloem

Zone of elongation

Cap of cells

Each year a tree's roots grow longer. Cells in the root's tip multiply and cause the zone of elongation to stretch lengthwise. This pushes the root tip further into the ground. A cap of cells protects the root tip from wear and tear. The tiny hairs growing out of the root draw in water and minerals from the soil. Root hairs only live for a few weeks at a time. In a root system, it is the younger roots which usually take in water and minerals. The older, tougher roots are used mainly for anchoring the tree.

Roots of the world

Trees in different parts of the world have unique ways of making the best of their environment. For example, roots in dry climates need to absorb as much water as possible, so they spread over a large area.

Banyan tree

This native of India and Sri Lanka grows hanging roots from its branches. These grow down to the ground, take root and become new trunks. In this way the tree gets bigger. The largest banyan has over 1,000 trunks.

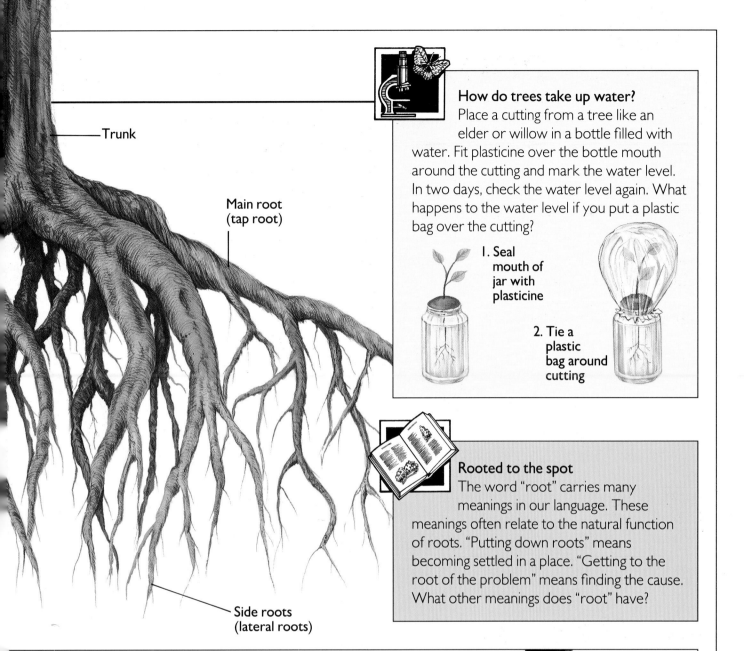

——— Trunk

Main root
(tap root)

Side roots
(lateral roots)

How do trees take up water?

Place a cutting from a tree like an elder or willow in a bottle filled with water. Fit plasticine over the bottle mouth around the cutting and mark the water level. In two days, check the water level again. What happens to the water level if you put a plastic bag over the cutting?

1. Seal mouth of jar with plasticine

2. Tie a plastic bag around cutting

Rooted to the spot

The word "root" carries many meanings in our language. These meanings often relate to the natural function of roots. "Putting down roots" means becoming settled in a place. "Getting to the root of the problem" means finding the cause. What other meanings does "root" have?

Apple trees

Apple trees grow in most temperate climates. Their roots are typical of most fruit-bearing trees. They do not grow very deep, but extend outwards forming millions of tiny rootlets.

Mangrove trees

Mangroves thrive along tropical coasts. Their roots are stilt-like to keep the tree secure in soft mud. Some of the roots grow upwards to get oxygen.

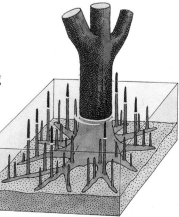

Spruce trees

Conifers can thrive in poor soil and cold climates. Their roots form a shallow disc shape just under the ground's surface.

Tropical rainforests

Trees in rainforests need only shallow root systems to absorb nutrients from the rich surface layer of soil.

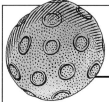

FLOWERS

The main function of a tree's flowers is to produce seeds which will grow into new trees. Flowers contain the tree's reproductive parts. They can be male or female or contain both male and female parts. Willows and poplars have male flowers on one tree and female on another. Most conifers have separate clusters of male and female flowers on the same tree. The wind carries pollen from the male flowers to fertilise the female flowers.

A flower's shape, colour and smell are designed to transfer male pollen grains to the female parts efficiently. Pollen is mainly transferred by insects or wind. Plants that rely on insect carriers have evolved brightly-coloured, sweetly-scented flowers that have a landing platform for insects. In warm climates, birds and bats transfer pollen when they fly from flower to flower sipping nectar.

APPLE BLOSSOM

Looking into flowers
Flowers vary from species to species in their shape, colour and size. Many trees in temperate (moderate, seasonal) climates are wind-pollinated, so they have unspectacular flowers because they do not rely on attracting insects.

Nikau palm flowers

Palms have small flowers which grow in large clusters. The pollinated flowers later develop into dates, coconuts or other fruits, depending on the species.

Walnut trees grow male hanging catkin flowers 5-10 cm long. The female flowers are rounded and stand upright.

Cones of Norway spruce

Pine flowers are very inconspicuous. The red or yellow clustered flowers develop into cones about a year after being fertilised.

Walnut catkin and flowers

There are many different kinds of magnolia trees, but all are known for their beautiful flowers which lure insects.

Magnolia flowers

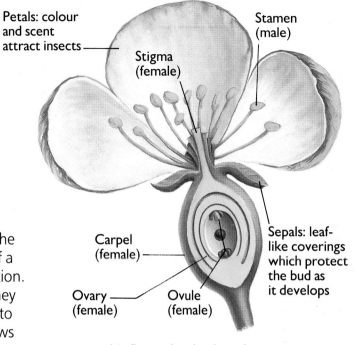

HONEYBEE

Petals: colour and scent attract insects

Stamen (male)

Stigma (female)

Carpel (female)

Sepals: leaf-like coverings which protect the bud as it develops

Ovary (female)

Ovule (female)

This flower has both male and female parts. Stamens produce millions of pollen grains at a time, each grain only 0.2 mm across.

Pollination

For a new seed to grow, male pollen grains must reach the female ovules, which are contained in the ovary in the carpel. This is called pollination. Even if a flower contains both male and female parts, it very rarely pollinates itself. Pollen usually travels from the male parts of a flower to the female parts of a different flower – this is called cross pollination. The design of a tree's flowers shows how they are pollinated. Willow catkins use the wind to carry their pollen. Their dangling shape allows the wind to scatter the pollen grains. Flowers pollinated by insects, such as bees and butterflies, attract them with their colour, smell and a store of sweet nectar to eat. Pollen sticks to the insects' legs and hairy backs, and is carried to the next flower they visit where it may join with an ovule.

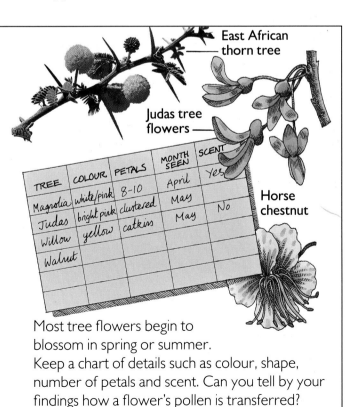

East African thorn tree

Judas tree flowers

Horse chestnut

TREE	COLOUR	PETALS	MONTH SEEN	SCENT
Magnolia	white/pink	8-10	April	Yes
Judas	bright pink	clustered	May	
Willow	yellow	catkins	May	No
Walnut				

Most tree flowers begin to blossom in spring or summer.
Keep a chart of details such as colour, shape, number of petals and scent. Can you tell by your findings how a flower's pollen is transferred?

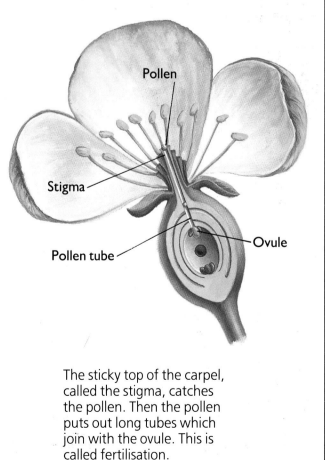

Pollen

Stigma

Pollen tube

Ovule

The sticky top of the carpel, called the stigma, catches the pollen. Then the pollen puts out long tubes which join with the ovule. This is called fertilisation.

FRUITS AND NUTS

Once fertilisation has taken place, the ovule develops into a seed. The ovary around it grows into a protective covering, called the fruit. There are many different forms of fruit – berries, nuts, pods, fleshy fruits, or, in the case of conifers, cones. The fruit protects the seeds and its shape helps them get carried to a suitable place to grow (see page 16). Fruits and nuts are often tasty and nutritious – they have evolved this way to attract animals, which will eat them and disperse the seeds.

A VARIETY OF FRUITS AND NUTS FROM TREES

Coconut

Grapefruit

Plum

Lemon

Pear

Walnut

Apple

Cob nut

1

2

A bee pollinates an apple blossom and fertilisation takes place (1). The flower dies, its job done (2). The ovary and base of the flower develop into a fleshy fruit around the apple seeds, or pips (3).

3

The first foods
Fruits and nuts were among humankind's first foods. Our early ancestors would gather these foods from the trees near them. However, depending on wild trees for food can be risky, so thousands of years ago people began to cultivate fruit-bearing trees from seeds. These small orchards supplied a more stable source of food than gathering could provide.

Ancient Egyptian orchard

Nuts to music

Nuts are large, dry, edible seeds with a strong husk (the fruit) protecting the flesh. This shell is usually discarded after the nut itself has been eaten. But some nutshells can make percussion instruments. On old radio shows, the two halves of a coconut shell were clapped together to make the sound of a horse's hooves. You can use them as a rhythm instrument. Smaller nuts, like pine kernels, can be enclosed in a plastic cup to make a shaker, or *maraca*.

Dispersal

Fruits are designed for various methods of dispersal. Trees cannot move, so seeds must be carried away from them, where there will not be as much competition for light and water.

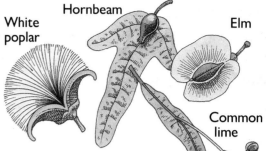

White poplar · Hornbeam · Elm · Common lime

Wind-blown

Some seeds have light wings which help them to travel. The wind carries them spinning through the air away from the tree. Others have white, downy parachutes which float in the wind.

Cherries

Carried by animals

Mammals and birds eat the soft fruits, berries and nuts of trees and drop the seeds to the ground. Some seeds can also pass through animals' digestive systems unharmed.

Bursting forth

The seeds of some trees are protected by pods until they ripen and the pods break open to release the seeds. The pods of different tree species vary in shape.

Laburnum

Water-borne

The white flesh of a coconut is actually a large seed. Its shell, covered with coarse fibres, acts as a float and carries the seed across the seas. When it reaches a beach it can take root and grow.

Coconut

Orange

Fig

Avocado

Horse chestnut

Loquat fruit

SEEDS TO SEEDLINGS

If a seed lands in a suitable place, with sufficient light and water, it will grow into a seedling. This process is called germination. It usually happens in spring, when the days get warmer and sunnier. Each seed contains the microscopic beginnings of a new tree and a store of food. Very few seeds survive, however. An oak tree may produce over 50,000 acorns a year. But only about two or three at most will grow into oak trees.

Sprouting

As the seed swells, the case cracks and the tree's first root (called the radicle) appears, followed by a shoot. In some species, the seed leaves (or cotyledons) unfold and force the seed case off. The emerging shoot is called the plumule, which will grow to become the trunk.

A PINE SEEDLING SPROUTS

Pine seed

Testa splits

Shoot

Radicle

Secondary roots

Parts of a seed

The seed is protected by a casing or coat, called the testa. There is often a scar on the seed which shows where it was attached to the ovary. The cotyledons are folded tightly inside the seed. Around them is a layer called the endosperm. It contains food on which the new tree will live until it can make its own. In some seeds, the cotyledons store the food which they have absorbed from the endosperm. When the seedling sprouts, these seed leaves will make food until the first true leaves grow. The cotyledons are often quite different in shape from what the tree's ordinary leaves will be.

Cotyledons

Endosperm

Testa

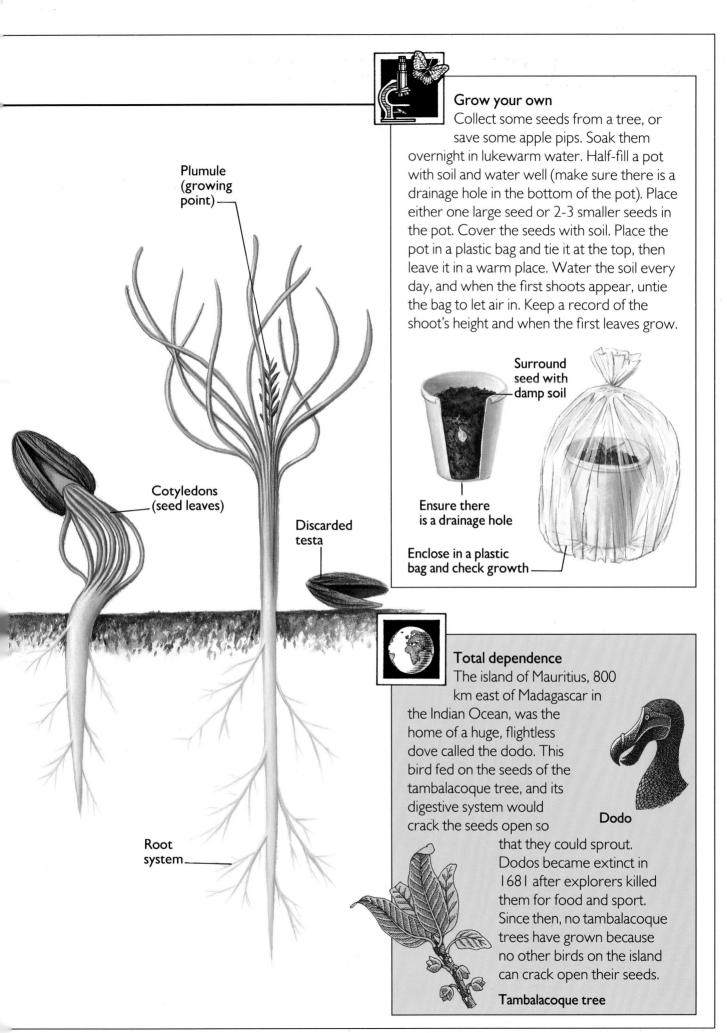

Plumule
(growing
point)

Cotyledons
(seed leaves)

Discarded
testa

Root
system

Grow your own

Collect some seeds from a tree, or save some apple pips. Soak them overnight in lukewarm water. Half-fill a pot with soil and water well (make sure there is a drainage hole in the bottom of the pot). Place either one large seed or 2-3 smaller seeds in the pot. Cover the seeds with soil. Place the pot in a plastic bag and tie it at the top, then leave it in a warm place. Water the soil every day, and when the first shoots appear, untie the bag to let air in. Keep a record of the shoot's height and when the first leaves grow.

Surround
seed with
damp soil

Ensure there
is a drainage hole

Enclose in a plastic
bag and check growth

Total dependence

The island of Mauritius, 800 km east of Madagascar in the Indian Ocean, was the home of a huge, flightless dove called the dodo. This bird fed on the seeds of the tambalacoque tree, and its digestive system would crack the seeds open so that they could sprout. Dodos became extinct in 1681 after explorers killed them for food and sport. Since then, no tambalacoque trees have grown because no other birds on the island can crack open their seeds.

Dodo

Tambalacoque tree

BUDS

In winter, the branches of deciduous trees are bare apart from tiny buds at the ends of the twigs. These buds contain new shoots, new leaves and sometimes new flowers. They do not grow during the winter. But as the warmer spring weather approaches, the buds burst open and the tree comes to life again. The leader bud, at the end of the twig, grows fastest. If it becomes damaged or dies, another bud grows by its side to take its place.

Counting the years
You can see where the previous year's leading bud was by the scar it leaves on the twig. This is called a girdle scar. There are also scars left where the previous year's leaves have fallen off. By counting the girdle scars you can determine the age of a twig or a small tree. Count down the twig from the present leading bud. Measure the distances between the girdle scars to see how much the twig has grown each year. The small buds growing to the side are dormant buds. They also contain leaves and flowers.

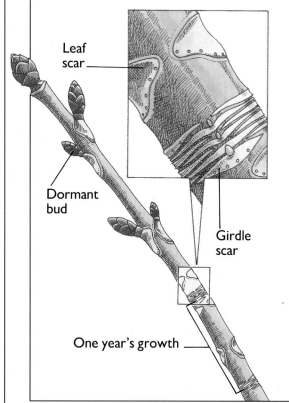

Leaf scar

Dormant bud

Girdle scar

One year's growth

OAK TWIG IN WINTER

Dormant bud

Leaf scar

Buds to branches
Every year a twig is built upon by the shoot from the leading bud. At the end of the growing season, a new bud develops. Gradually, a branch will form in this way.

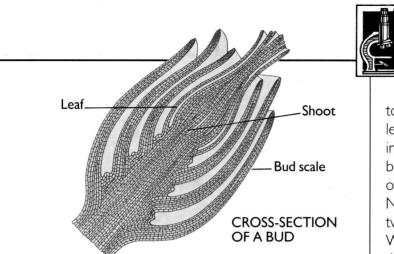

Leaf

Shoot

Bud scale

CROSS-SECTION OF A BUD

Inside a bud

The tiny beginnings of the new shoot, leaves and flowers are packed closely together inside the bud. They are protected from the winter cold, from animal attacks and from drying out by thick, overlapping bud scales. These are sometimes sticky. If there are no bud scales, the bud may be covered in tiny hairs. In spring, the warm weather makes the new shoot and leaves swell. The bud bursts open as they push the bud scales apart.

HAZEL BRANCH IN SUMMER

Bud

Bud identification

You can identify deciduous trees by their buds, which are much easier to see in winter when the tree has lost its leaves. Different species have great variation in their twigs and buds. Observe how the buds are arranged on the twig; are they in opposite pairs or do they occur on their own? Note the colour and shape of the bud and twig. Is the bud covered with hair or scales? Write down your observations and compare them with a tree identification book to determine the species of the tree.

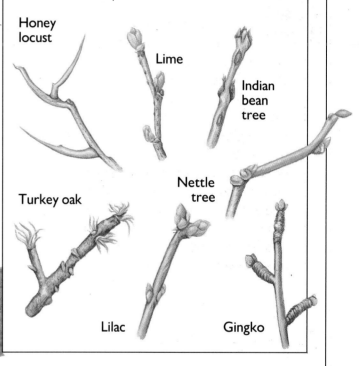

Honey locust

Lime

Indian bean tree

Turkey oak

Nettle tree

Lilac

Gingko

Tree pests

The spruce budworm was once one of the most destructive insects in North America. Now it is controlled by pesticides. The budworm is the caterpillar stage of a moth which lays its eggs on fir and spruce trees. When the caterpillars hatch they eat the buds and other parts of the tree, destroying it. The pest once spread rapidly through the huge timber plantations of spruce and fir, ruining hectares of trees. At one stage the budworm problem was so bad that the large numbers of adult moths looked like a snowstorm when they took to the air.

HOW A TREE GROWS

Each year a tree grows thicker, taller and, in some cases, bushier. Its girth increases as a new layer of wood is added to its trunk. This makes the trunk stronger so that it can support the weight of new branches. These grow longer as cells at the branch tips multiply. The tree's roots spread further underground to anchor the tree firmly. The tree also grows new leaves.

Cambium
The cambium produces a new ring of sapwood each year. It makes the trunk and branches thicker and stronger.

Sapwood
Sapwood is mainly made of living cells. It contains tiny tubes which carry water and sap around the tree (see pages 22-23).

Heartwood
Heartwood is the hard, darker coloured dead wood in the middle of the trunk. It supports the tree.

SCOTS PINE

A tree's main areas of growth are at the tips of its branches, around its trunk and at its root tips. Deciduous trees grow new leaves every year. Evergreen trees may replace their leaves or needles gradually every two or three years.

Tree records
The tallest tree species on Earth is the redwood of California. It has been known for a redwood to grow to 113 metres tall. The fastest growing tree is the acacia tree of Malaysia, which can grow 11 metres in three months. A bristlecone pine in California is the oldest tree – 4,600 years old.

Acacia

Redwood

1939
On 3 September, World War II breaks out after Hitler's Germany invades Poland.

1969
The American astronaut, Neil Armstrong, becomes the first man to step on the moon.

1885
Two German inventors, Daimler and Benz, pioneer the automobile.

1990
What important events happened during this year?

Rays
Rays carry food and water sideways through the sapwood.

Annual growth rings

Each year, the layer of cambium inside the tree's trunk produces a ring of new wood. This pushes the cambium outwards and makes the trunk thicker. These annual rings can be counted to find out how old a tree is. They are also a record of past weather conditions. Wide rings grow in years with plenty of rain. In dry years, the rings are narrow and close together.

There are no annual rings inside a palm tree trunk. Palm trunks contain a mass of unorganised fibres. They do not contain cambium to make new wood, so the trunk never gets wider, only taller.

Making a bonsai tree

Bonsais are dwarf trees which are planted in Japanese and Chinese ornamental gardens. Although real bonsais are skilfully sculpted, you can use this short cut to make your own. You will need to get a dwarf conifer, a shallow tray, compost, scissors, wire and clippers. Trim the roots of the tree. Then wind wire around the roots to restrict root growth. Plant the tree in the tray and trim the branches to the shape you want. Ensure the tree gets water and light.

3 Snip out branches

2 Bind the root ball with wire

1 Trim the roots

THE TREE TRUNK

The trunk holds a tree up so that its leaves can make full use of the sunlight, its flowers can be pollinated and its seeds scattered. The trunk also contains tubes which carry water and sap (minerals and food) around the tree. For protection, the trunk is covered in a tough, outer layer, called bark. This protects the tree from attack by animals and fungi, and also insulates it against extreme heat or cold.

SILVER BIRCH

Measure it up

To estimate a tree's height, one person (A) stands at the base of the tree. Another (B) moves away holding a pencil at arm's length. When the pencil appears the same height as A, estimate how many pencil-lengths would match the height of the tree. Then multiply A's actual height by this number to get the tree's approximate height.

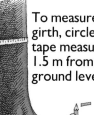

To measure girth, circle a tape measure 1.5 m from ground level.

A

B

Measuring height

Wood down the ages

Throughout human history, wood has been vital in improving people's lives. From rubbing sticks together to make fire, to felling trees to build shelter, you can find wood everywhere in history.

Papermaking

Paper was invented in China 2,500 years ago. Wood pulp is now the main material in paper.

Totem poles

The Native American peoples of the Pacific Northwest recorded events by elaborately carving stories and symbols in wood.

Ancient Egypt

This coffin was carved from wood for an Egyptian priestess around 1050 BC.

EUCALYPTUS

INSIDE A TRUNK

Bark

Cork
cambium
(layer of
living cells
which
divide to
produce
bark)

Xylem

Phloem

Inside the trunk, a system of tubes called xylem carries water and minerals upwards from the roots to the leaves. Tubes called phloem carry food in the form of sugary sap from the leaves to the rest of the tree. The bark protects this life-support system.

Trees can sometimes be identified by the pattern their bark makes. It may be deeply cracked or split, or peeling off in papery strips. Small holes in the bark, called lenticels, allow the tree to take in oxygen and carbon dioxide. Trees also breathe through their leaves.

Adapting to habitat

The environment in which a tree grows affects the way it develops. Individual trees have to adapt to the conditions where they live. If a strong wind consistently blows in one direction, from the sea, for instance, a tree's trunk and branches will grow in this direction. The strong, bitterly cold Arctic winds twist and stunt the branches of the Arctic beech into strange shapes. Where trees grow close together, their trunks remain narrow and their branches grow near the top to reach the light. Examine the trees around you, and see if you can find ways they have adapted to survive in their habitat.

Arctic beech

Shipbuilding

Boats have been built from wood for thousands of years. The Greeks (500 B.C.) had an extensive fleet of wooden ships. The great sailing ships of the 15–16th century, like this Dutch galleon, were wooden. Metal was not used until the 1800s.

WHERE DO TREES GROW?

Trees grow all over the world, even in the harshest of conditions. They live in deserts, on mountains, in jungles and in the icy cold. Since trees can make their own food, they are not restricted to places where food can be found, as animals are. They do, however, need sunlight and water wherever they live. Many species have developed special features which help them to survive in a particular habitat.

Desert and scrubland

Desert trees face the problem of getting enough water to live on. Baobab trees store water in their swollen trunks for use in times of drought. As they use up the water, their trunks shrink.

Mountain

Some mountain trees, such as dwarf willows and dwarf conifers, grow very close to the ground. This keeps them out of the biting winds which howl down the mountainside. They may be short enough to step over – only a few centimetres high. These trees are given the nickname *krummholz*, or "elfin wood".

Northern pine forest

A huge band of pine forest stretches across the top of North America, Siberia and Scandinavia. Conifers form crowded and shady forests. They can survive even where the sunlight is weak.

Mangrove swamps

Bands of mangrove trees grow in tropical estuaries, where rivers meet the sea. They have to cope with large amounts of salt which would normally kill most trees. Mangrove trees' roots have special adaptations which filter the salt out of the water they take in.

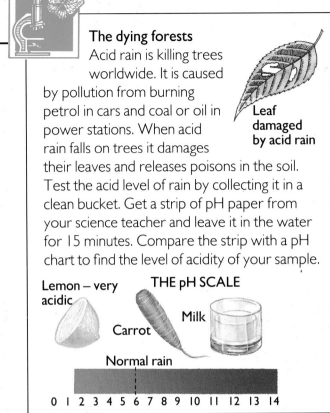

The dying forests

Acid rain is killing trees worldwide. It is caused by pollution from burning petrol in cars and coal or oil in power stations. When acid rain falls on trees it damages their leaves and releases poisons in the soil. Test the acid level of rain by collecting it in a clean bucket. Get a strip of pH paper from your science teacher and leave it in the water for 15 minutes. Compare the strip with a pH chart to find the level of acidity of your sample.

Leaf damaged by acid rain

THE pH SCALE

Lemon – very acidic

Carrot

Milk

Normal rain

| 0 | 1 | 2 | 3 | 4 | 5 | 6 | 7 | 8 | 9 | 10 | 11 | 12 | 13 | 14 |

Tropical rainforests

Rainforest trees grow in dense groups. They have to compete for sunlight, and can grow up to 50 m tall to catch the sun. Rainforest trees absorb all the nutrients from the soil. When they are felled the soil is left with so few nutrients that it is difficult for other vegetation to grow back.

The world's biomes

The Earth can be divided into regions based on the kind of trees they support. These areas, called biomes, are largely determined by climate: temperature and rainfall are the main influences on what kinds of trees and plants grow in an area. Soil type also affects vegetation, because it is the soil that supplies nutrients for plants. The map below shows the world's major biomes.

Tropical deciduous seasonal

Arid grassland

Desert

Savanna

Evergreen tropical

Cool coniferous

Mediterranean woodland

Deciduous temperate

Evergreen temperate

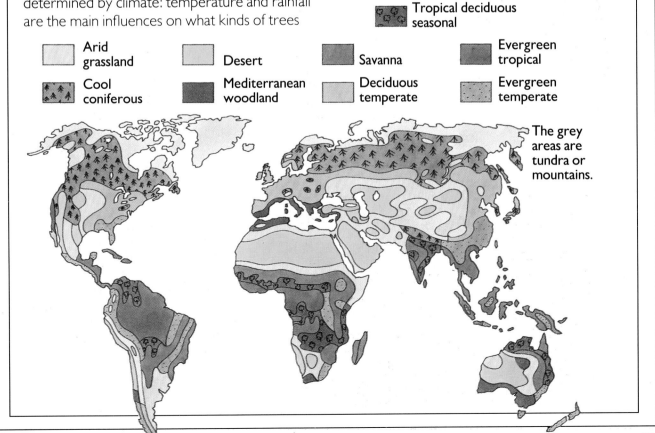

The grey areas are tundra or mountains.

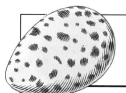

TREES AS HABITATS

A single tree may be home to hundreds or even thousands of living things. It offers shelter from predators, protection from bad weather, a food supply and a place to nest or hibernate. Every part of the tree is used. Birds nest in its branches or in holes in its trunk. Insects, woodlice and spiders crawl among its roots. Some insects burrow under the bark. Fungi grow on its trunk or feed on the leaf litter around its base. Many kinds of mammals live in trees, from koalas in Australian eucalyptus woods, to squirrels in temperate forests.

Woodpeckers are good examples of creatures which are well adapted to woodland life. Many species have sharp, pointed beaks for chiselling away at the tree bark to get at the insect grubs underneath. They pull them out with their long, sticky tongues. Their feet are adapted for gripping and climbing. Their stiff tails support them as they climb. Woodpeckers nest in holes in the tree's trunk or in branches.

What's in a tree?
A tree contains a wealth of life. One oak might support as many as 400 species. Investigate a tree, noting down in a scrapbook any evidence of animal or plant life. Examine a tree closely, looking around its base and at its trunk and branches. To observe birds and other animals, sit away from the tree and use binoculars if possible.

Bark stripped by deer

Sometimes you can find evidence that animals have been using the tree. Bark is stripped off where deer rub their antlers against the trunk. Squirrels, voles and rabbits gnaw at young bark as a source of nutrients.

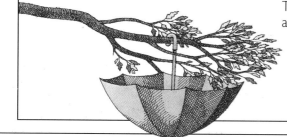

To look at a tree's insects, attach an open umbrella under a branch and shake the tree. Carefully identify what you have dislodged, then release all the creatures back to the tree safely.

Take photos

Disappearing habitat

Tropical rainforests lie in a belt around the Equator. Over half the world's species of plants and animals live in these ancient forests. However, they are being cleared for timber, cattle ranching and farming. The rainforests in parts of Southeast Asia have been almost totally destroyed. Some scientists estimate that one species is made extinct every half hour as a result of rainforest clearance. Animals such as the sloth and lemur rely on the trees of the rainforest for survival. When the forests are felled, there is no place for these species to go. People also lose their homes as a result of the destruction.

The result of rainforest burning in the Amazon

GILA WOODPECKER

Lark

Leaf skeleton

Insect gall

Moth

Wasp

Fungus

Fungi and plants like vines and creepers grow on trees, and insects like caterpillars feed on the leaves. Insects can cause abnormal growths called galls on tree branches. Decayed leaf skeletons litter the soil around the tree's base. Keep a record of what you see, but make sure you never harm the tree or its occupants in any way. Take impressions of the bark by taping paper onto the trunk and rubbing it with a crayon. If you find any fallen leaves, press them out and stick them into your scrapbook. Sketch the tree's flowers and fruit.

OAK

SPRING Buds open. Birds starting to nest. Some fungus around the base.

SUMMER Flowering. Blossoms covered in pollen. Holes in leaves from caterpillars feeding. Baby birds hatched.

AUTUMN Leaves changing colour. Nut husks below tree. Squirrels seen.

HOW WE USE TREES

Trees are essential to our lives, as they supply us with much of the oxygen we need to breathe (see page 7). They also provide us with many of the things we use every day – food, medicines, wood for furniture and buildings, paper and rubber (see left). Aspirin is derived from willow bark, cork comes from cork oak bark and paper is made from wood pulp. Coffee and chocolate start life as the fruits of tropical trees. Colas are flavoured with the cola nut from a West African tree.

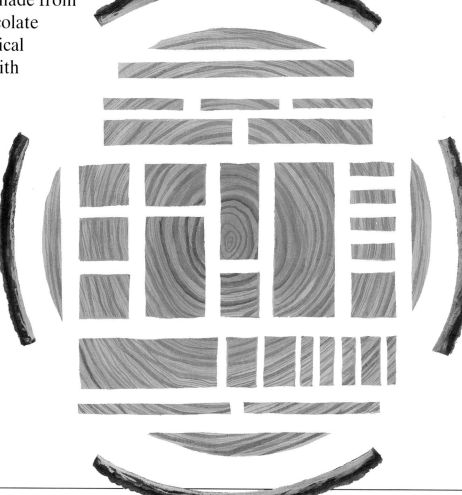

Logs are cut into planks at a sawmill. They are sawn up in special ways to get the maximum amount of usable wood from them. The fresh, "green" planks have to be dried out, or seasoned, before they can be used. Otherwise they might warp or shrink. Nothing is wasted. Small wood chips are pulped for paper or made into particle board.

Making paper

You can recycle paper at home. Soak some newspapers overnight. Then drain off the water and mix the papers into a mush. Put this pulp into a bowl and add an equal amount of water. Then strain the pulp through a sieve. Place the mixture onto a flat cloth and press it out with your hands or a rolling pin. Put another cloth over the top, and repeat the whole process to make more layers.

Around the home

You may not realise how many things in your home originally came from trees. Coal, for instance, is the remains of trees and plants which were compressed under the ground for millions of years. Many fruits and spices come from trees. Write down everything you can find which is a product of a tree. Then make a bar chart showing the quantities of each item.

Books

Furniture

Matches

Cinnamon

Cork

Coal

Hardwood and softwood

There are two distinct types of wood: softwood (from conifers) and hardwood (from broadleaves). These labels can be misleading; the wood from the yew tree is extremely hard although it comes from a softwood tree. Balsa wood is quite soft although the tree is considered a hardwood. Softwoods grow more quickly than most hardwoods and their wood is used for timber and paper. Hardwoods like teak, oak and ebony are used to make high quality furniture. Because hardwood trees generally have to grow for at least 30 years before they can be harvested, it takes a long time to replace them when they are felled.

When you are finished, put a plastic bag on the final cloth and then add heavy books to press the paper down. Leave it for several hours, until the paper is dry. You can get interesting effects by adding powdered paint to the pulp, or leaves to your paper before you press it out.

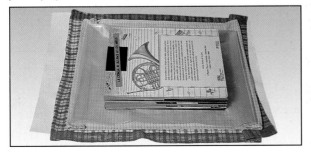

Wooden instruments

People have used wood to make musical instruments for thousands of years. This is because it is durable, easy to work with and also makes a fine resonant sound. One wooden row of pipes dates back to 2000 BC. Drums made from hollowed wood are common to most cultures. Harps are made from wood, as are lutes and guitars. Violins are made from three types of wood: the stringside is made from a softwood like pine or spruce, the back from a harder wood like maple, and the fingerboard from a very hard wood, usually ebony. Piano keys are also inlaid with ebony, for durability.

Ancient coin showing pan pipes

Drum

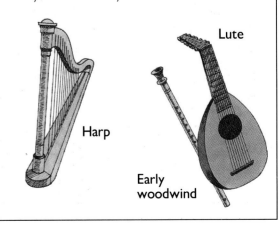

Lute

Harp

Early woodwind

SPOTTER'S GUIDE

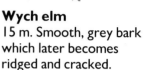

English oak
20 m. Grey, ridged bark and wide spreading branches. Acorns.

Common beech
30 m. Smooth, grey bark. Dense, sometimes purple, leaves.

Norway maple
20 m. Ridged, grey bark, small, yellow flowers. Winged seeds.

Wych elm
15 m. Smooth, grey bark which later becomes ridged and cracked.

Common ash
40 m. Elongated shape. Leaves come out after flowers in spring.

Weeping willow
15 m. Red-brown bark and drooping shape. Long, narrow leaves.

Silver birch
20 m. Smooth, white, flaking bark. Drooping branches, catkin flowers.

Fig
6 m. Soft, grey bark. Small, spreading shape. Edible fruit.

Black walnut
30 m. Brown-black bark, catkin flowers. Hollow twigs. Edible nuts.

Scots pine
35 m. Scaly, rusty-red bark, bare trunk. Blue-green needles.

European larch
40 m. Yellow-brown to grey bark; loses needles in winter.

Douglas fir
60 m. Dark brown bark, hanging shaggy cones. Used for timber.

Western red cedar
30 m. Orangish bark, branches curve upwards. Tiny, flower-like cones.

Yew
20 m. Deep red bark, gnarled trunk. Highly poisonous.

Common juniper
6 m. Grey-brown bark, shrubby shape. Blue berry-like cones.

Italian cypress
25 m. Tall, thin shape, grey bark. Round, grey, woody cones.

GLOSSARY

Acid rain Rain turned into a weak solution of sulphuric or nitric acid by pollution from factories, power stations and vehicle exhausts. Carried by the wind, it falls on forests and lakes, killing trees and fish.

Adaptation Special features which help a tree to survive in a particular place. For example, desert baobab trees have stretchy trunks for storing water in times of drought.

Biome A large region of the Earth, based on its climate and the type of trees and other plants that can grow there.

Carpel The female reproductive part of a flower which contains the ovary.

Chlorophyll A green pigment (colouring) in a tree's leaves. It uses energy from sunlight to turn carbon dioxide, water and minerals into a simple type of food, called sap.

Deciduous Trees which shed their leaves in winter, when the temperature falls and there is not enough sunlight to make food.

Dispersal The way in which a tree's pollen is carried to another tree for fertilisation, or the way fruits and seeds travel to a suitable place to grow. They may be dispersed by wind, water or by animals.

Evergreen Trees which keep their leaves throughout the year. Evergreen trees include most conifers.

Evolution The development of living things into new species which are better adapted to the changing environment. This takes place over thousands or millions of years as the individual plants which have the best characteristics for their habitat survive and reproduce while others die out.

Extinction The permanent loss of a species from the planet.

Fertilisation After pollination, a male pollen grain joins with a female ovule to produce a new seed. This is called fertilisation.

Germination The way in which a seed grows into a seedling (a new plant).

Habitat The type of place a tree lives in, such as a forest, mountain or desert.

Hardwood Wood from broadleaved trees.

Pests Insects, fungi or viruses which can seriously damage or kill trees.

Phloem A system of tubes inside a tree which carries food, called sap, from the leaves to the rest of the tree.

Photosynthesis The process by which a tree makes its own food. Using energy from sunlight it combines carbon dioxide from the air, with water and minerals from the soil, into a simple, sugary food. During this process the tree takes in oxygen and carbon dioxide and expels oxygen, which humans and other animals need to live.

Pollination The transfer of male pollen grains to the female ovaries, to form new seeds. Most trees reproduce by cross pollination – the pollen is taken from one flower to another flower.

Softwood Wood from conifer trees.

Stamens The male reproductive parts of a flower. They produce millions of pollen grains at a time.

Transpiration The way in which trees lose water through tiny holes, called stomata, found mainly on a leaf's underside.

Xylem A system of tubes inside a tree which carries water and minerals upwards from the roots to the leaves.

INDEX

Photographic credits:
Cover: top middle: Bruce Coleman Limited; top right: Planet Earth Pictures; bottom left: Frank Spooner Pictures; bottom right: Roger Vlitos.

All the pictures inside the book have been supplied by Bruce Coleman Limited apart from pages: title page and pages 4 top left, 7, 8 top, 9 top, 14-15, 19, 20-21 all, 26 right, 27 bottom left and right, 28 bottom left, middle and right, 29 top left, middle and right and 29 bottom: Roger Vlitos; pages 4 right and 23: Frank Lane Pictures; pages 9 bottom, 22 bottom left and 23 bottom: Mary Evans Picture Library; page 22 top: Planet Earth Pictures; page 22 bottom right and 29 middle: The British Museum.